LEAD
THE WAY

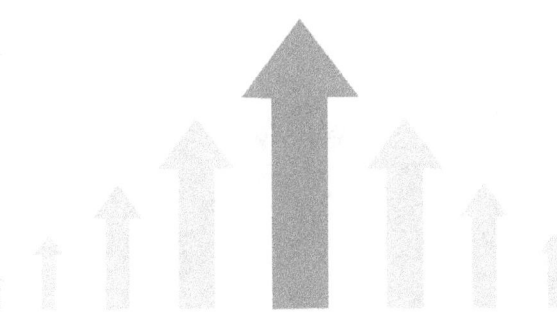

LEAD
THE WAY
A GUIDE FOR STUDENT LEADERS
Primary School Edition

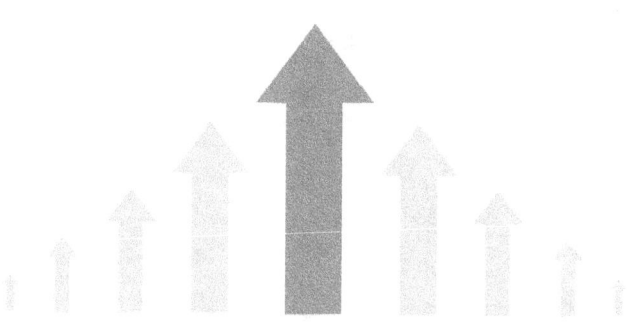

LUKE McKENNA

Copyright © 2025 by Luke McKenna

All rights reserved. Except as permitted under the Australian Copyright Act 1968, no part of the publication be reproduced, stored in a retrieval system, communicated or transmitted in any form or by any means - electronic, mechanical, photocopying, recording or otherwise without the prior written of the publisher.

Prepublication Data Services available on request from the National Library of Australia.

ISBN: 978-0-9943866-6-3

Edited by Rebecca Hood
Typesetting and Design by Mortuza Karzon

Published with the assistance of Lightning Source.

Contents

INTRODUCTION FOR STUDENT LEADERS 6

PART 1: PERSONAL SHIFTS 10

PERSONAL SHIFT #1-FROM REACTIVE TO PROACTIVE 12

PERSONAL SHIFT #2-FROM BELOW THE LINE TO ABOVE THE LINE THINKING AND BEHAVIOUR 15

PERSONAL SHIFT #3-FOCUS ON YOUR CIRCLE OF INFLUENCE, NOT JUST YOUR CIRCLE OF CONCERN 19

PERSONAL SHIFT #4-FROM "HAVING" TO "BEING" 22

PERSONAL SHIFT #5-FROM PLAYING A SHORT GAME TO PLAYING A LONG GAME 24

PERSONAL SHIFT #6-FROM ORDINARY TO EXTRAORDINARY 26

PERSONAL SHIFT #7-FROM WORDS TO ACTIONS 28

PERSONAL SHIFT #8-FROM ENTITLEMENT TO GRATITUDE 30

PERSONAL SHIFT #9-FROM ME TO WE 32

PERSONAL SHIFT #10-FROM PAST AND PRESENT SELF TO FUTURE SELF 34

PERSONAL SHIFT #11-FROM FORCE TO STRENGTH 36

PART 2: LEADERSHIP SHIFTS 38

LEADERSHIFT #1-FROM BEING SERVED TO SERVING OTHERS 40

LEADERSHIFT #2-FROM POSITION AND POWER TO EXAMPLE AND INFLUENCE 42

LEADERSHIFT #3-FROM GOING UP TO GROWING UP 45

LEADERSHIFT #4-FROM WIN/LOSE TO WIN/WIN 47

LEADERSHIFT #5-FROM DRAGGING OTHERS DOWN TO LIFTING OTHERS UP 49

LEADERSHIFT #6-FROM UNIFORMITY TO UNITY 52

LEADERSHIFT #7-FROM DOING WHAT YOU ENJOY TO DOING WHAT NEEDS TO BE DONE 55

BECOMING A LEADER WORTH FOLLOWING 57

CONCLUDING REMARKS: A VISION FOR TOMORROW'S LEADERS 59

ABOUT UNLEASHING PERSONAL POTENTIAL (UPP) 61

INTRODUCTION FOR STUDENT LEADERS

WHY READ THIS BOOK?

Do you want to make a difference in your school, your class, or even at home? This book is for you! It will show you small changes you can make to become a stronger, kinder, and more positive leader.

Being a leader isn't just about helping others — it's about learning to lead yourself first. When you practice the ideas in this book, you'll make better choices, be true to your values, and inspire the people around you.

Some people think being a leader means being popular or the "boss." But that's not real leadership. Real leaders care about others, stay humble, and do the right thing even when nobody is watching.

By reading this book, you'll learn how to be a leader people can trust and respect.

WHO IS THIS BOOK FOR?

This book is for primary school student leaders — whether you wear a badge or not. You might be a school captain, sports leader, peer mentor, or someone who simply wants to make your school a better place.

Being a leader isn't about having a badge or title. It's about how you act and how you treat people every day. By learning to lead yourself first, you'll become ready to lead others with courage and care.

School is more than just learning maths, spelling, or science. It's also where you practice being the kind of person you want to become. The choices you make now shape your future.

WHERE DOES IT START?

It starts with you. Don't wait for someone else to step up. If you want things to get better — in your class, team, or even your family — you need to do your part. You have more power than you think!

A famous leader, Margaret Mead, once said:

> *"Never doubt that a small group of thoughtful, committed people can change the world. In fact, it's the only thing that ever has."*

Even in primary school, you can start making a positive difference.

LEADERSHIP THAT LASTS

Some people only want to be leaders so they can have power or attention. But the best leaders care about serving others and helping their team. When they do this, their influence grows — because real leaders inspire others to lead too.

This is how great school cultures are built: leaders growing more leaders.

WHAT DOES A "SHIFT" MEAN?

This book explains a number of Personal Shifts and Leadership Shifts that we can all make.

A shift is a small but powerful change in the way you think or act. Imagine two planes taking off from the same airport. If one plane turns just a little off course, and continues slightly off course, they'll end up in very different places. That's what shifts are like in life.

Your future is shaped by the small shifts you make every day — how you treat people, how you react to challenges, and the choices you make when things get hard.

CHOOSE YOUR PAIN: DISCIPLINE OR REGRET

Here's something to think about: in life, you can't avoid all pain. But you can choose between two types of pain:

- **The pain of discipline** — like getting up early to go to training, studying when you'd rather play, or helping at home when you're tired.
- **The pain of regret** — like wishing you had trained, studied, or helped after it's too late.

Great leaders choose the pain of discipline more often. It's not always fun in the moment, but it makes you stronger and more confident later. Poor leaders choose the pain of regret. They try to take shortcuts, but then have to suffer the consequences of those actions later on.

Choose the pain of discipline.

LEADERS SHOW THE WAY

The best leaders don't just talk about what to do — they show it. They live it. You can't expect others to follow you if you're not willing to go first.

It's easy to understand leadership ideas. The hard part is living them every day. But even one small shift can set you apart, because leadership is rare.

THE TWO PARTS OF THIS BOOK

This book has two parts:

1. **Personal Shifts** – changes in how you think and act, so you can lead yourself well.
2. **Leadership Shifts** – changes that help you lead others better, with kindness, courage, and care.

LEAD YOURSELF FIRST

If you don't lead yourself, others won't want to follow. If you're always complaining, blaming, or being unkind, why would anyone want to copy you?

The best leaders aren't perfect, but they are always learning and growing. They are kind, thoughtful, and determined. They make small, daily shifts that add up to big changes.

That's what this book is about — becoming a better person and a leader worth following.

PART 1: PERSONAL SHIFTS

Leading From the Inside Out

Before you can lead others, you need to learn to lead yourself. These **Personal Shifts** are small changes in how you think and act that will help you grow as a leader.

Here's what you'll learn in this part of the book:

PERSONAL SHIFT #1 — From Reactive to Proactive
Don't just react to what happens — choose your response and take control of your actions.

PERSONAL SHIFT #2 — From Below the Line to Above the Line
Instead of blaming or making excuses, take responsibility and make positive choices.

PERSONAL SHIFT #3 — From Circle of Concern to Circle of Influence
Focus your energy on the things you can change, not the things you can't.

PERSONAL SHIFT #4 — From Having to Being
Don't just wish for good results — become the kind of person who makes them happen.

PERSONAL SHIFT #5 — From Playing a Short Game to Playing a Long Game
Don't just look for quick rewards — build habits that bring success over time.

PERSONAL SHIFT #6 — From Ordinary to Extraordinary
Choose to give your best effort every day, even in the little things.

PERSONAL SHIFT #7 — From Words to Actions
Make sure your words match your actions. Live the values you talk about.

PERSONAL SHIFT #8 — From Entitlement to Gratitude
Stop expecting everything to go your way. Instead, learn to be thankful for what you have.

PERSONAL SHIFT #9 — From Me to We
Great leaders don't focus only on themselves. They work with others and help the team succeed.

PERSONAL SHIFT #10 — From Past and Present Self to Future Self
Think about the kind of person you want to be in the future — and make choices now that move you in that direction.

PERSONAL SHIFT #11 — From Force to Strength
Don't push or control others. Lead with calm confidence and respect, so people want to follow you.

PERSONAL SHIFT #1-
From Reactive to Proactive

LIVING BY DEFAULT OR BY DESIGN

Some students just drift along at school — waiting to see what happens and letting things control them. That's called *living by default*.

Other students make choices about who they want to be and how they want to act. That's called *living by design*.

As a student leader, you get to choose: Will you wait for things to happen, or will you help make them happen?

Great leaders don't just react. They act first. They set a positive example and make things better for others.

WHAT DOES PROACTIVE MEAN?

Being proactive means *choosing your response* instead of just reacting.

It means:

- Taking action when someone is left out.
- Encouraging your team when group work is hard.

- Staying calm and respectful when something doesn't go your way.

Proactive people don't blame others or wait for someone else to fix the problem. They stop, think, and choose the best response.

THE POWER OF CHOICE

Every day you face choices:

- Do I complain about group work, or do I help my team?
- Do I ignore a lonely student, or do I invite them to join in?
- Do I talk badly about someone, or do I encourage them?

You always have the power to choose. That's what makes you a leader.

REACTIVE VS PROACTIVE

Reactive people often say things like:

- "There's nothing I can do."
- "That's just the way I am."
- "It's not my fault."

When we think like that, we give away our power.

But proactive people understand *response-ability* — responsibility is the ability to choose our response.

Instead of:
Event = Outcome

Think:
Event + My Response = Outcome

Example: If a friend says something unkind, you could get angry and argue. OR… you could pause and ask, "Are you okay? That didn't sound like you." The event is the same, but your choice changes the outcome.

BE A LEADER BY DESIGN

Leaders live by design, not by default. Each day, ask yourself:

- Who do I want to be today?
- What kind of leader do I want to be?
- How will I choose to respond?

When you make these choices, you take back your power — and show others what real leadership looks like.

QUESTIONS TO THINK ABOUT:

- When do I usually react instead of respond?
- What's one area where I could make a better choice this week?
- What's one proactive decision I could make today?

PERSONAL SHIFT #2-
From Below the Line to Above the Line Thinking and Behaviour

↑↑↑

UNDERSTANDING THE LINE

Imagine a line across a page. The way you think and act can be **below the line or above the line.**

- **Below the Line** means blaming others, making excuses, or pretending nothing is your fault. (We call this BED thinking: **Blame, Excuses, Denial**).
- **Above the Line** means taking responsibility, owning your choices, and stepping up. (We call this OAR thinking: **Ownership, Accountability, Responsibility**).

Leaders choose to live above the line.

WHAT BELOW THE LINE LOOKS LIKE

Sometimes people don't even notice they're living below the line. They might say:

- "It's not my fault."
- "It's not fair."

- "The teacher didn't tell me."

But blaming and excusing doesn't change anything. You can't control other people — you can only control your own response.

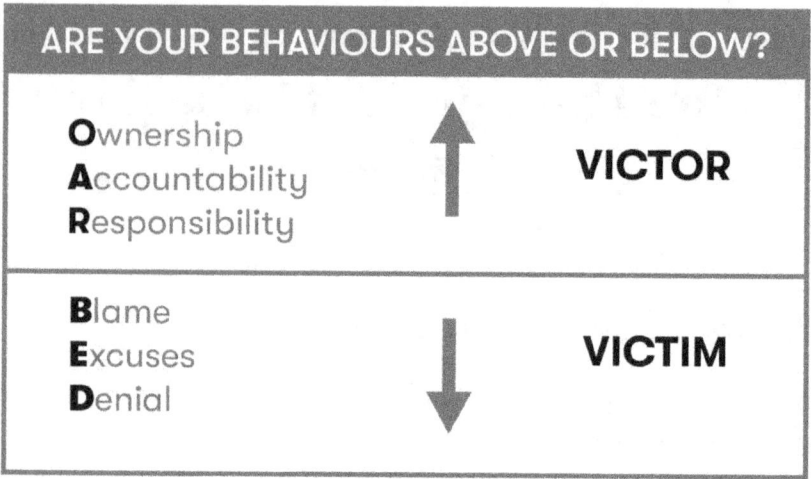

WHAT ABOVE THE LINE LOOKS LIKE

When you live above the line, you own your actions.

Example: You forget to bring the sports gear for your team.

- **Below the line:** "No one reminded me! It's not my fault."
- **Above the line:** "I forgot. That was on me. I'll make sure it's ready next time."

Taking ownership doesn't mean you're perfect. It just means you're honest, responsible, and ready to grow.

ABOVE THE LINE
Thinking & Behaviours

- Accountable
- See Possibilities
- Ownership
- Find Better Ways
- Seek & Provide Feedback
- See It
- Look for Solutions
- Hope
- Take Action
- Make Choices

BELOW THE LINE
Thinking & Behaviours

- Excuses
- Deny
- Victim
- See Failure
- Find Fault
- Block Feedback
- No Control
- Ignore
- Blame
- Wait for Others

WHY ABOVE THE LINE IS BETTER

Above the line thinking can be harder in the moment — but it's much more rewarding in the long run.

Here's a simple process to follow:

1. See it.
2. Own it.
3. Solve it.
4. Do it.

Bad leaders blame and avoid. Good leaders take responsibility and act.

THE WINDOW AND THE MIRROR

At UPP, we talk about this idea:

- When things go well → **Look out the window.** Give credit to your team.
- When things don't go well → **Look in the mirror.** Ask, "What could I have done better?"

Weak leaders do the opposite — they hog the praise and push away the blame. Strong leaders understand the window and the mirror, and know when to use each one.

TWO QUICK STORIES

- **Sam and Jordan:** Both fail a test. Jordan blames the teacher (below the line). Sam asks for help and studies harder (above the line). Next time, Sam improves. Jordan doesn't.
- **Alex and Taylor:** Both get dropped from the sports team. Taylor blames the coach (below the line). Alex trains harder and asks for feedback (above the line). Soon Alex is back on the team.

Same problem, different mindset, very different outcomes.

QUESTIONS TO THINK ABOUT:

- When do I fall into blame or excuses?
- What's one area where I could take more ownership this week?
- Who do I know that shows above the line behaviour? What can I learn from them?

PERSONAL SHIFT #3-
Focus on Your Circle of Influence, Not Just Your Circle of Concern

WHAT CAN YOU CONTROL?

One of the biggest lessons for leaders is learning the difference between what you *can control* and what you *can't*.

- **Circle of Influence:** the things you can do something about — like your effort in class, how you treat friends, the way you practice for sport, or how you speak to your teacher.
- **Circle of Concern:** the things that affect you, but you cannot control — like the weather, how the other team plays, or whether someone else is in a bad mood.

What I Can't Control
- Someone Else's Decisions
- How Others Treat Me
- Height
- Skin Color
- Death
- Others Taking Care of Themselves
- Who Likes Me
- Others Being Kind
- Who Loves Me
- Past Mistakes
- Others Being Honest
- If Someone Else Keeps Trying
- Others Forgiving Me
- Others Apologising to Me
- Weather
- Others Asking for Help

What I Can Control
- Doing my Homework
- Respecting Property
- Being Kind
- Being Accountable
- Studying for Tests
- The Friends I Choose to Have
- My Decisions
- Forgiving
- How I Respond to Challenges
- Trying Again
- How I Spend My Free Time
- Doing My Chores
- Taking Care of Myself
- Being Honest
- Asking for Help
- How I Respond to Other
- Apologising

WHY IT MATTERS

If you spend your energy on your Circle of Concern, you'll feel frustrated and powerless. For example:

- Complaining about the rain won't stop the rain.
- Worrying about the other team won't change how they play.

But if you put your energy into your Circle of Influence, you grow stronger. For example:

- If sport is cancelled, you can do a workout at home.
- If someone is distracting in class, you can stay focused and be a role model.

Leaders focus on what they *can* control.

A HELPFUL QUESTION

When something goes wrong, ask yourself:

- "Can I control this?" If yes → do something about it. If no → let it go and move forward.

QUESTIONS TO THINK ABOUT:

- What's one thing I often worry about that I can't change?
- What's something in my influence I can act on this week?

PERSONAL SHIFT #4 - From "Having" to "Being"

BE → DO → HAVE

Most people think life works like this: *"If I have the right things, then I can do what I want, and then I'll be happy."*

But leaders know it works the other way:

1. **Be** the right kind of person.
2. **Do** the right actions.
3. **Have** the results you want.

Examples:

- Be respectful → Do kind actions → Have strong friendships.
- Be organised → Do regular homework → Have good grades.
- Be a team player → Do extra encouragement → Have a strong team.

WHY THIS MATTERS

Everyone wants to *have* good stuff — but not everyone wants to *be* disciplined or *do* the hard work. Leaders start with who they are becoming, not what they want to get.

Think about a great musician. They don't just suddenly "have" talent. First, they become dedicated, then they *practice* every day, and only then do they *have* the skill to perform well.

QUESTIONS TO THINK ABOUT:

- What do I want to have in my life right now?
- What do I need to do to get there?
- Who do I need to be to make those actions possible?

PERSONAL SHIFT #5-
From Playing a Short Game to Playing a Long Game

QUICK WINS

Sometimes we just want the short game: the quick praise, the easy reward, the "well done" from others. It feels good, but it doesn't last.

Examples of the short game:

- Rushing homework to get it done fast.
- Cutting corners in sport training.
- Doing just enough to get noticed.

LONG GAME

The long game is about building habits that last. It's harder, but it creates real success.

Examples of the long game:

- Studying properly so you understand the work long-term.
- Practising sport skills regularly, even when no one's watching.

- Choosing kindness and honesty, even when it's not popular.

PLANTING A TREE

A Chinese proverb says:

> *"The best time to plant a tree was 20 years ago. The second-best time is now."*

Imagine planting a seed. At first, it's just a tiny sprout. You might even wonder if anything's happening. But over time, with sunlight, rain, and care, it becomes a tall tree that gives shade, fruit, and beauty.

The short game wants fruit **now**. The long game is willing to wait, knowing the reward will come.

WHY IT MATTERS FOR LEADERS

Great student leaders think beyond today. They make choices that build trust and respect over time.

QUESTION TO THINK ABOUT:

- What small daily action could I keep doing that will help me in the future?

PERSONAL SHIFT #6-
From Ordinary to Extraordinary

ORDINARY VS EXTRAORDINARY

Ordinary means doing just enough. Extraordinary means choosing to give your best, even in the little things.

Extraordinary leaders:

- Show up on time.
- Keep their word.
- Speak kindly when tired.
- Own their mistakes.
- Bring positive energy to their class or team.

WHY IT MATTERS

Extraordinary doesn't mean perfect. It means choosing to raise the bar. If you always settle for "just enough," people won't follow you. But if you keep choosing your best, people notice — and they trust you.

THE EXTRA MILE

Great leaders go beyond what's asked.

Most people don't do this. That's why extraordinary leaders stand out.

That's the extra mile.

Ordinary stops at "done." Extraordinary asks, "What more can I do to help?"

- If you're setting up chairs, check that the rows are neat.
- If you lead a group for an event, thank the people who helped behind the scenes.
- If you're walking past rubbish, pick it up even if it's not "your job."

QUESTIONS TO THINK ABOUT:

- How can I do ordinary tasks with excellence?
- What's one way I can go the extra mile this week?

PERSONAL SHIFT #7- From Words to Actions

TALK VS WALK

It's easy to say the right words. But people follow what you do, not what you say.

Imagine a student leader says, "We should all respect each other," but then they ignore classmates or speak rudely. Will anyone really listen?

ACTIONS SHOW VALUES

Every school has values like Respect or Responsibility. But values don't mean much unless you live them.

- If you're honest, people will notice.
- If you're kind, people will feel it.
- If you're responsible, people will trust you.

Your actions prove your values more than any speech.

WHY THIS MATTERS FOR LEADERS

Student leaders are role models. People copy what they see — not just what they hear. If you want kindness, honesty, and respect in your school, you need to model it first.

QUESTIONS TO THINK ABOUT:

- Do my actions match my words?
- What value do I want to live out more often?

PERSONAL SHIFT #8-
From Entitlement to Gratitude

COMPLAINING VS THANKFUL

Some people expect things to always go their way. If they don't, they complain or blame others. This is called entitlement.

Grateful people are different. Instead of saying, "Why didn't I get that?" they say, "I'm thankful for what I do have." Gratitude makes life brighter, and people enjoy being around thankful leaders more than complaining ones.

WHY GRATITUDE WORKS

Our brains notice what we look for. If we look for problems, we'll always find them. But if we look for the good, we'll notice more positives every day.

Example: You can complain about homework, or you can be thankful that you have the chance to learn and grow.

SIMPLE GRATITUDE HABITS

- Start or finish each day by writing 3 things you're grateful for.
- Say "thank you" more often — to friends, teachers, family.
- When things go wrong, ask: "What's one good thing here I can still be thankful for?"

WHY LEADERS CHOOSE GRATITUDE

Leaders who show gratitude:

- Encourage others by noticing their efforts.
- Spread positivity to their class or team.
- Become more resilient when challenges come.

QUESTIONS TO THINK ABOUT:

- What's one thing in my life I sometimes take for granted?
- Who can I thank today for something they've done?

PERSONAL SHIFT #9-
From Me to We

ALONE VS TOGETHER

You can go fast alone, but you can go further together. Leaders understand that working with others creates bigger and better results than working alone.

BIG POTENTIAL VS SMALL POTENTIAL

Shawn Achor, a happiness researcher, talks about small potential (what you achieve by yourself) and big potential (what you achieve with others). Big potential always wins.

Example: In a class project, one person might do okay on their own. But when everyone contributes — sharing ideas, helping each other — the group creates something far greater.

WHY "WE" MATTERS

- Others have skills you don't.
- Working as a team builds trust and stronger friendships.
- Helping others first often means they'll help you later.

THE WISDOM OF THE CROWD

This idea shows that a group of diverse people often makes better decisions than one expert alone. A famous example comes from a 1906 country fair in England. A contest asked 800 people to guess the weight of a large bull. The guesses were all over the place, but when the average of all of the guesses was taken, it was just 1% off the real weight of the bull. The collective group was smarter than any single person.

Together, we tend to make better decisions and achieve more.

You'll achieve more when you shift your focus from just me to we. When you focus on helping others, your own life improves as well.

QUESTIONS TO THINK ABOUT:

- How can I include others more often instead of doing things myself?
- How can I lift up a teammate or classmate this week?

PERSONAL SHIFT #10 –
From Past and Present Self to Future Self

PICTURE YOUR FUTURE

Your future self is the person you are becoming. Leaders focus not only on who they are now, but on who they want to be.

Example:

- If you want to be a confident speaker in high school, you might start practising in class now.
- If you dream of being a great athlete, you'll train consistently even when you are not with the rest of your team.

WHY IT MATTERS

If you don't imagine a good future, you're less likely to prepare for it. But if you picture a bright, exciting future, your choices today will match that vision.

A HELPFUL EXERCISE

Each month, ask yourself:

1. Where am I right now?
2. What went well this month?
3. What do I want to improve next month?
4. What do I hope to achieve in the next year?
5. Who do I want to be in 3–5 years?

GROWING FORWARD

Great leaders always aim to make their future bigger than their past. Each day is a chance to take one more step toward your best self.

QUESTIONS TO THINK ABOUT:

- What kind of person do I want to be in 5 years?
- What small choice today can help me become that person?

PERSONAL SHIFT #11- From Force to Strength

FORCE VS STRENGTH

- **Force:** trying to push, control, or scare others into doing something. Often leads to conflict.
- **Strength:** leading calmly, kindly, and confidently. Strength earns trust and inspires others.

WHY IT MATTERS

Leaders who use force might get short-term results, but people follow them out of fear, not respect. Leaders who use strength create long-lasting trust and teamwork.

WHAT STRENGTH LOOKS LIKE

Staying calm when things go wrong.

- Treating others with respect, even when you disagree.
- Listening to ideas and valuing different opinions.
- Leading by example, not just by telling others what to do.

A REAL EXAMPLE

Imagine two captains:

- **Captain A** yells and blames when the team loses.
- **Captain B** encourages the team, asks how they can improve, and keeps working hard.

Which team would you rather play on? Which leader would you rather follow? That's the difference between force and strength.

QUESTIONS TO THINK ABOUT:

- Do I push people to get my way, or do I inspire them to follow?
- How can I lead with more calm strength this week?

PART 2: LEADERSHIP SHIFTS

Becoming a Real Leader

People often have different ideas about what a leader really is. Sometimes, when we think about leaders, we imagine people who are rich, powerful, or always in charge. They might look strong on the outside, but sometimes they can be selfish or only care about themselves.

Other times, we see leaders who are calm, kind, and ready to help others. That can feel confusing when you're starting out as a leader, because you might wonder: *Which kind of leader should I be?*

Some students don't want to be leaders because they've seen bad examples — leaders who were bossy, unfair, or made poor choices. This can make leadership seem unappealing, even though real leadership is actually something positive and exciting. The truth is, many people have the wrong picture of what leadership is. Real leadership isn't about being the boss or getting attention. It's about making a difference for others.

In this part of the book, we'll explore Leadership Shifts — small but powerful changes in the way we think about leadership. These shifts helped me grow as a leader, and they can help you too. First, they changed the way I thought. Then, when I put them into action, I noticed real changes in how I led others.

These **Leadership Shifts** will challenge some of the myths about leadership and guide you toward becoming the kind of leader that people want to follow.

Leadership Shifts You'll Learn

LEADERSHIFT #1
From being served to serving others
True leaders don't expect special treatment. Instead, they step up to help, support, and care for others.

LEADERSHIFT #2
From position and power to example and influence
Leadership isn't about wearing a badge or having authority. It's about setting a good example and having a positive impact.

LEADERSHIFT #3
From going up to growing up
Leadership isn't about perks or rewards. It's about becoming more responsible, patient, and willing to serve others.

LEADERSHIFT #4
From Win / Lose to Win / Win
Great leaders find ways for everyone to succeed, not just themselves.

LEADERSHIFT #5
From dragging others down to lifting others up
Real leaders encourage and build people up — not tear them down.

LEADERSHIFT #6
From uniformity to unity
Leadership doesn't mean making everyone the same. It means bringing people together and celebrating differences.

LEADERSHIFT #7
From doing what you enjoy to doing what needs to be done
Leaders don't just choose the easy or fun jobs. They step up and do what needs to be done — even when it's hard.

LEADERSHIFT #1-
From Being Served to Serving Others

WHAT MANY PEOPLE THINK

Sometimes, people think being a leader means being "the boss" or getting special treatment. They expect others to serve them. But that's not real leadership.

WHAT REAL LEADERS DO

Real leaders serve their team. They help, support, and encourage others. They carry some of the load and make things easier for everyone.

Example: A good sports captain doesn't just give speeches — they might also help set up the gear, encourage teammates, or check that everyone's ready before the game.

THE WATER BOTTLE STORY

When I was in high school, I was chosen to be the captain of my indoor soccer team. I felt proud and excited. I imagined myself giving big speeches, motivating the team, and leading us to victory.

But on the very first day, my coach gave me one simple job: **fill up the water bottles for the team before every game.**

At first, I was confused. I thought, *'Really? That's it? I'm the captain — shouldn't I be leading the team out on the court, not carrying bottles?'*

But over time, I realised something important. Filling the bottles wasn't just about water. It was about serving the team. It showed that I cared about my teammates and wanted them to be ready to play their best. It reminded me that leadership isn't about looking important — it's about helping others succeed.

Sometimes leadership looks like giving a speech, but often it looks like doing a small job that makes a big difference. Great leaders serve in both the big and the little ways.

WHY IT MATTERS

Leaders who expect to be served are not respected. Leaders who serve others earn trust and loyalty.

QUESTIONS TO THINK ABOUT:

- Who can I serve today in a small but important way?
- How can I make life easier for my team or class?

LEADERSHIFT #2-

From Position and Power to Example and Influence

LEADERSHIP ISN'T ABOUT A BADGE

You don't need a badge, title, or special position to be a leader. Leadership is about the example you set and the way you influence others.

MY STORY: WHEN A SIMPLE 'GOOD MORNING' MADE A DIFFERENCE

When I was at school, I was given the role of school captain. I got the badge, gave speeches, met important people, raised money and did all the official things. At the time, I thought that was what leadership was all about.

Years later, I was surprised to learn from a friend that his younger brother thought I was a "really great guy." I asked my friend what I'd done to earn that praise, expecting he'd say something about my speeches or the things I did as school captain.

My friend told me that most days I said "good morning" to his younger brother with a smile — and sometimes, I was the only person outside his class who did.

That small, simple act made a bigger impact than any title or speech. It showed me that leadership is about the little things — respect, kindness, and showing you care. It doesn't require a title, a speech or a badge. What really matters is how you treat each person, every day. And anyone can do a good job of that.

After all, you don't need a badge to be a leader.

WHY INFLUENCE MATTERS

Your influence is the effect you have on others. When you are positive, respectful, and kind, you encourage others to be the same.

Examples of positive influence:

- Including someone who's alone at lunch.
- Working hard in class and encouraging others.
- Speaking up when something isn't fair.

HOW DO YOU BUILD INFLUENCE AS A LEADER?

You earn influence by showing up every day as someone people can trust and respect. This means living out the personal shifts you've been learning, like being responsible, proactive, and respectful in all that you do.

At UPP, we use something called the **ASPIRE framework** to explain what good leadership looks like:

- *ACTION* – Step up and do what needs to be done, instead of waiting for someone else.
- *SERVICE* – Help others because you care, not just to get a reward.
- *PERSISTENCE* – Keep going and don't give up, even when things feel tough.
- *INFLUENCE* – Use your words and actions to make a positive difference.
- *RESPECT* – Treat everyone fairly, even when it's not easy.
- *ENCOURAGEMENT* – Cheer people on and support those around you.

When you choose to live these values, people naturally notice. They see that you care, that you are honest, and that you can be trusted. That's how you build true influence — others will be more likely to follow your lead because they respect the way you act.

QUESTIONS TO THINK ABOUT:

- How can I lead by example this week?
- What small action could inspire others around me?

LEADERSHIFT #3-
From Going Up to Growing Up

THE PERKS OF LEADERSHIP

Leadership sometimes comes with extra privileges: a badge, recognition, or being noticed. It can feel exciting to "go up."

BUT REAL LEADERSHIP MEANS GROWING UP

Good leaders don't just enjoy the perks — they grow in character and responsibility. That means:

- Showing up on time.
- Taking responsibility when things go wrong.
- Being kind and fair to everyone.
- Listening carefully to others.
- Staying steady when things are hard.

MOVING FROM "WHAT CAN I GET?" TO "HOW CAN I GROW?"

Early in my leadership journey, I focused on what I could get — the titles, the recognition, the rewards. But I soon realised leadership is really about growing up: becoming a stronger, wiser, kinder person who can help others succeed.

Now, my goal is to keep growing — learning, listening, supporting, and improving — so I can lead by example, make a more positive contribution to the world and help our team grow too.

WHY IT MATTERS

Leaders who only want perks don't last. Leaders who grow stronger, wiser, and kinder make a lasting difference.

QUESTIONS TO THINK ABOUT:

- How am I growing as a leader?
- What responsibility can I take on this week to help my team?

LEADERSHIFT #4- From Win/Lose to Win/Win

THE WIN/LOSE MINDSET

Some people think that if one person wins, someone else must lose. You might see this in sports, games, or even school projects. But in leadership, that mindset doesn't help.

THE WIN/WIN WAY

Great leaders look for solutions where everyone benefits. That's called *win/win*.

Example: If your class is planning a fun day, a win/lose mindset might mean one group pushes only their ideas. But a win/win approach means listening to everyone and creating a plan that includes parts from different people — so the whole class enjoys it.

THE POWER OF WORKING TOGETHER

In nature, some animals have special partnerships where both benefit. For example, a fish and a shrimp work as a team: the shrimp digs a safe home in the sand where both live, and the fish warns the shrimp of danger. Both get something important, so they both win.

We can do the same in our relationships and teams. When we work together, help each other, and look for solutions that benefit everyone, the whole group becomes stronger.

WHY IT MATTERS FOR LEADERS

Win/win builds trust, teamwork, and fairness. If you always try to win at the cost of others, people won't want to follow you.

QUESTIONS TO THINK ABOUT:

- How can I make sure everyone feels included and valued?
- What's one way I could turn a win/lose situation into a win/win this week?

LEADERSHIFT #5-

From Dragging Others Down to Lifting Others Up

"Strong people don't put others down. They lift them up."

Michael P. Watson

HOW DO YOU REACT WHEN SOMEONE ELSE SUCCEEDS?

When someone in your class, team, or group does something great, how do you feel? Do you feel happy for them, or do you feel a little jealous or worried? Sometimes, when people feel unsure about themselves, they might try to put others down to feel better. But that doesn't help anyone — it only makes things worse.

Remember: someone else's success doesn't take away from your chances to succeed. And putting others down won't make you better or stronger.

WHY LIFTING OTHERS UP MATTERS

There's a famous saying by Robert Ingersoll: **"We rise by lifting others."** This means that when you help others succeed and feel good about themselves, you also become stronger as a person and as a leader.

Think about it like this: if a rising tide lifts all the boats in the harbour, when you lift someone else up, it lifts everyone — including you.

REAL TEAMWORK IS ABOUT SUPPORT

A few years ago, I was talking with some leaders in our team. We were thinking about who might be ready for a new challenge or responsibility. Instead of competing against each other, two team members actually spoke highly of each other — they lifted each other up with respect and support.

That's what real leaders do. They cheer on others and help their teammates grow.

WHY GIVING COMPLIMENTS IS POWERFUL

You might notice that when you give someone a genuine compliment or say "great job," it feels good for both of you. Compliments show that you notice and appreciate the good in others — and that makes people want to support you back.

Good leaders are generous with praise. They don't just criticise or compete — they encourage and build others up.

YOUR CHALLENGE FOR TODAY

Can you find two people to give a real compliment to? It could be a teammate, a classmate, or someone you know. Say something kind and specific — like "I really liked how you helped out in class today" or "You did a great job in that game!"

Great leaders build others up — and when you do, you all rise together.

QUESTIONS TO THINK ABOUT:

- Who can I encourage today with a compliment?
- How can I help my classmates or teammates feel stronger?

LEADERSHIFT #6-
From Uniformity to Unity

WHY BEING THE SAME ISN'T THE GOAL

Sometimes, people think leaders should only work with people who are just like them — who think the same way or act the same. But great leaders know that's a mistake. Good leaders actually look for people who have different skills and ideas, because those differences make the whole team stronger.

WHAT UNITY REALLY MEANS

Unity means working together toward the same goal while celebrating differences. Everyone brings their own gifts and talents, and that variety makes the group stronger.

Example: In a soccer team, not everyone plays the same role. Some players are great at defending, some are strong midfielders who pass the ball well, and others are skilled at scoring goals. The team succeeds because each person uses their unique strengths. If everyone only wanted to score, the team would fall apart. Winning comes from working together and valuing each role.

DIFFERENT TYPES OF LEADERS BRING DIFFERENT STRENGTHS

In our leadership workshops, we talk about three kinds of leaders — and everyone is a mix of these, but some people are stronger in one area than others:

- **Prophet leaders:** These leaders are full of ideas. They love to brainstorm and dream about new possibilities. They are creative and excited about the future, and their ideas inspire others. They're the "light bulb" people who spark innovation.
- **Planner leaders:** These leaders are the organisers. They focus on the details, make plans, create schedules, and get things done. They think about who needs to do what, when, and how. They love ticking off tasks and making sure things run smoothly.
- **People leaders:** These leaders care deeply about others. They listen well, support people, and help make sure everyone feels included. They build strong friendships and encourage their teammates. People tend to follow them because of the trust they build.

EVERYONE BRINGS SOMETHING IMPORTANT

No one is perfect or has all these skills — not even the best leaders. The smartest leaders know their own strengths and also know when to ask others for help. By doing this, they help other people grow and make the whole team better.

WHAT DOES THIS LOOK LIKE IN REAL LIFE?

Imagine you and your friends are planning a fundraiser for a cause you care about.

- The **prophet leaders** come up with ideas for the fundraiser. Maybe it's a bake sale, a sports event, or a talent show.
- The **planner leaders** work out the details — where it will be, what you need to do, when everything will happen, and who will help.
- The **people leaders** make sure everyone on the team knows their role, feels included, and is excited to be part of the event.

All three types of leadership are needed to make the fundraiser a success.

WHY THIS MATTERS TO YOU

Sometimes, you might be tempted to only listen to people who think like you or agree with you. But when you appreciate and use the different strengths of everyone around you, your team can achieve much more.

Great leadership isn't about everyone being the same. It's about **working together, celebrating differences, and uniting strengths** to make something amazing happen.

WHY LEADERS CHOOSE UNITY

Great leaders:

- Value different ideas.
- Include people who might be left out.
- Celebrate strengths in others.

QUESTIONS TO THINK ABOUT:

- Who in my class or team has different strengths than me?
- How can I make sure everyone feels included and important?

LEADERSHIFT #7-

From Doing What You Enjoy to Doing What Needs to Be Done

THE EASY WAY

It's tempting to only do the jobs we enjoy — like leading a game, speaking on stage, or being in charge. But leadership isn't about what's fun for you.

THE LEADER'S WAY

Leaders step up to do what needs to be done — even if it's boring, hard, or behind the scenes.

Examples:

- Picking up rubbish even if no one else notices.
- Helping set up chairs when others want to talk.
- Doing extra practice when you'd rather rest.

THE ALL BLACKS AND "SWEEPING THE SHEDS"

In his book *Legacy*, James Kerr shares a story about the All Blacks, New Zealand's famous rugby team. They are one of the best teams in the world, with lots of superstars and championships.

But here's the interesting part: after every game, the players themselves clean up the locker room. They sweep the floor, throw away trash, and tidy up. And it's not the newest or least experienced players who do this — it's the senior players, the team's leaders.

Even though they have big contracts and are super important, they don't think any job is too small or beneath them. If something needs to be done, the real leaders do it.

WHAT THIS MEANS FOR YOU

If you want to grow as a leader — in your family, your school, or any group you belong to — look for the things that need doing. Step up and do those things.

This is what makes a leader stand out: focusing on the needs of others and the team, not just on what's easiest or most fun.

WHY IT MATTERS

If leaders only do the easy or fun jobs, the team suffers. Real leaders show they can be trusted with *all* jobs — big or small, fun or tough.

QUESTIONS TO THINK ABOUT:

- What's one job at school I don't usually enjoy, but I could do this week to serve others?
- How can I set the example by doing the hard or boring things well?

Becoming a Leader Worth Following

WHAT MAKES A LEADER WORTH FOLLOWING?

People don't follow leaders just because of a badge or title. They follow leaders they respect, trust, and admire.

A leader worth following is:

- **Kind** – They care about others and include everyone.
- **Honest** – They tell the truth and keep their promises.
- **Courageous** – They do the right thing, even when it's hard.
- **Hardworking** – They show effort and commitment every day.

WHY THIS MATTERS

If you only care about yourself, people may follow you for a little while, but not for long. If you care about others, they will want to follow you — not because they have to, but because they *want* to.

YOUR CHALLENGE

Every day, ask yourself:

- Am I being the kind of leader I would want to follow?

If the answer is yes, keep going. If the answer is no, make a small shift. That's how you grow.

And that's how you Lead the Way.

About Unleashing Personal Potential (UPP)

At UPP, our mission is simple: to help every student be their best.

We run workshops, camps, and programs for schools all across Australia. Since 2015, we've worked with more than 400,000 students, helping them learn, grow, and lead with kindness, courage, and excellence.

We believe every young person has potential — and our goal is to help you unlock it.

ABOUT THE AUTHOR

Luke McKenna is the founder of UPP. He's a teacher, school leader, and author who loves helping students and schools thrive.

Luke has studied business, education, and leadership, and he continues to speak and write about how young people can grow as leaders and live with purpose.

He lives in Brisbane with his wife, Laura, and their three children.

A NOTE OF GRATITUDE

I am so thankful — for the amazing teachers I've worked with, the dedicated UPP team who make this work possible, and most of all, my family, who always support and encourage me.

It's an honour to share this journey with you.

Lead with heart. Lead with courage. And always lift others as you rise.

Your leadership journey starts now.

www.ingramcontent.com/pod-product-compliance
Lightning Source LLC
Chambersburg PA
CBHW050330010526
44119CB00050B/740